THE GRANDMA MOSES AMERICAN SONGBOOK

THE OLD CHECKERED HOUSE

SNOWBALLING

Paintings by Grandma Moses

Music arranged for piano and guitar by Dan Fox

Harry N. Abrams, Inc., Publishers
New York

The Publishers wish to thank Jane Kallir and Hildegard Bachert of the Galerie St. Etienne for their generous cooperation and Jim Levas of The New York Public Library (Music Research Division) for his assistance.

Music engraving by Hal Leonard Publishing Corporation, Milwaukee, Wisconsin

Editors:
Ruth Eisenstein
Lois Brown

Designers:
Betsy Perlman and Tina Strasberg

Library of Congress Cataloging in Publication Data
Main entry under title:

The Grandma Moses American songbook.

~~For voice and piano; with chord symbols~~.
~~Includes index~~.
1. Music—United States. 2. Songs, ~~English—United States.~~ ~~3.~~ Folk-songs, English—United States. ~~4.~~ Music, Popular (Songs, etc.)—~~United States.~~ I. Moses, Grandma, 1860–1961, ill. II. Fox, Dan. arr.
~~M1629.G69~~3 1985 85–750799
ISBN 0–8109–0990–1

Printed and bound in Japan

On the Cover: THE BARN DANCE

DOWN MEMORY LANE

ALL FOR LOVE

THE BIRDS AND THE BEASTS WERE THERE

UPWARD AND ONWARD

BUT ONCE A YEAR

OF THEE I SING

A LITTLE WORK

A LITTLE PLAY

THE VILLAGE CLOCK

DOWN MEMORY LANE

AULD LANG SYNE

Words and music by Robert Burns

Dm
B♭
C7
F
days of auld lang syne? For
F
C/F
F
auld lang syne, my dear, for auld lang
mf - f
B♭/F
F
Dm
C
Gm/B♭
A7
syne; We'll take a cup of kind - ness yet for
Dm
B♭
C7
1
F
B♭
2
F
auld lang syne. For syne.

GRANDFATHER'S CLOCK

Words and music by Henry C. Work

In watching its pendulum swing to and fro,
Many hours had he spent while a boy;
And in childhood and manhood the
clock seemed to know,
And to share both his grief and his joy.
For it struck twenty-four when he entered
at the door,
With a blooming and beautiful bride.

My grandfather said that of those he could hire,
Not a servant so faithful he found;
For it wasted no time, and had but one desire,
At the close of each week to be wound.
And it kept in its place, not a frown upon its face,
And its hands never hung by its side.

It rang an alarm in the dead of the night,
An alarm that for years had been dumb;
And we knew that his spirit was pluming its flight,
That his hour of departure had come.
Still the clock kept the time, with a soft
and muffled chime,
As we silently stood by his side.

HOME! SWEET HOME!

Bb7
Eb
skies seems to hal - low us there, which
Ab
Eb
Bb7
Eb
seek thru the world is ne'er met with else - where.
Eb
Bb7
Cm
Bb
Eb
Ab
Eb
Home! Home! Sweet, sweet home! Be it ev - er so
Bb7
Eb
hum - ble, There's no place like home.

IN A LITTLE RED BARN

Words and music by Joe Young, Jean Schwartz, and Milton Ager

C B7 C Cm G
barn - yard where the farm - yard folks are pal - ly,
Em/G G+ G A9-5 A9 Adim A7
Let me dil - ly dal - ly all the live long
D7 G
day. I'm a Hoo - sier who's blue, thru and
E+ E7 A7
thru, and my heart is pin - ing For the

D7
B7
Em
syc - a - more trees where the Wa - bash breez - es play.
C6/E
E♭7
G/D
B7
What's more I'm pin - ing for a yel - low moon that's
Em
Em/D
C♯dim
G
E7
shin - ing
On a lit - tle red barn on a
3
L.H.
A7
D7
G
G7
Gdim
Cm6
G
farm down In - di - an - a way.

PUMPKINS

THE SPRING IN EVENING

JUST A SONG AT TWILIGHT

Words by G. Clifton Bingham
Music by J.L. Molloy

IN THE GLOAMING

Words by Meta Orred
Music by Annie Fortescue Harrison (Lady Arthur Hill)

F
F7
Bb
F7
soft - ly go. Where the winds are sob - bing
Bb
G7/B
F/C
Bb
F
G7-5
C7
faint - ly, with a gen - tle un - known woe,
F
C7
C#dim
Dm
Will you think of me and love me,
Gm
F/C
C7
F
As you did once long a - go.

LISTEN TO THE MOCKING BIRD

Words by Alice Hawthorne (pseud. of Septimus Winner)

2
G
D7
lies. Lis - ten to the mock - ing - bird, lis - ten to the
G
D7
mock - ing - bird, The mock - ing - bird still sing - ing o'er her
G
D7
grave. Lis - ten to the mock - ing - bird, lis - ten to the
G
C
D7
G
mock-ing - bird, Still sing - ing where the weep-ing wil - lows wave.

LITTLE BROWN CHURCH IN THE VALE

Words and music by W.S. Pitts

F7
Bb
lit - tle brown church in the vale.
come to the church in the vale."
optional background
Oh
F7
Come to the church in the wild - wood, Oh
come come come come come come come come come come come come
mp
Bb
Eb
come to the church in the dale.
No spot is so dear to my
come come come come come come come...
mf
Bb
Eb
F7
Bb
(D.C.)
child - hood As the lit - tle brown church in the vale.
19

LONG, LONG AGO

Words and music by Thomas Haynes Bayly

C7
F
light - ed to hear, long, long a - go, long a - go.
ne'er would for - get, long, long a - go, long a - go.
lips, have been praised long, long a - go, long a - go.
C7
F
Now you are come, all my grief is re - moved;
Then to all oth - ers my smile you pre - ferred;
But by long ab - sence your truth has been tried;
C7
F
Let me for - get that so long you have rov'd. Let me be - lieve that you
Love, when you spoke, gave a charm to each word. Still my heart trea - sures the
Still, to your ac - cents, I lis - ten with pride. Blest as I was when I
C7
F
love as you loved, long, long a - go, long a - go.
prais - es I heard, long, long a - go, long a - go.
sat by your side long, long a - go, long a - go.

THE OLD OAKEN BUCKET

Words by Samuel Woodworth
Music by G. Kiall Mark

Additional lyrics:

That moss covered bucket I hailed as a treasure,
For often at noon, when returned from the field.
I found it a source of an exquisite pleasure,
The purest and sweetest that nature can yield.
How ardent I seized it, with hands that were glowing,
And quick to the white pebbled bottom it fell.
Then soon, with the emblem of truth overflowing,
And dripping with coolness, it rose from the well.
Chorus:

How sweet from the green, mossy brim to receive it,
As poised on the curb it inclined to my lips!
Not a full blushing goblet could tempt me to leave it,
Tho' filled with the nectar that Jupiter sips.
And now, far removed from the loved habitation,
The tear of regret will intrusively swell,
As fancy reverts to my father's plantation,
And sighs for the bucket that hung in the well.
Chorus:

THE QUILTING PARTY

THE QUILTING BEE

SUNRISE, SUNSET

Words by Sheldon Harnick
Music by Jerry Bock

D7+5(♭9)
Gm
D7
they? When did she get to be a
side. Place the gold ring a-round her
(as before)
Gm
D7
Gm
beau - ty? When did he grow to be so tall?
fin - ger, Share the sweet wine and break the glass;
G7
Cm
G7
Cm
A7
Was - n't it yes - ter - day when they were
Soon the full cir - cle will have come to
D
D7
D+
Gm
Cm6
small?
pass.
Sun - rise,
mf
mp

Gm D7 Gm Cm6 Gm D7 Gm D7
sun - set, sun - rise, sun - set, swift - ly flow the
Gm G7 Cm7 F7
days, Seed - lings turn o - ver - night to
Bbmaj7 Ebmaj7 Am7(no 5th) D7
sun - flow'rs blos - som - ing e - ven as we
Gm Cm6 Gm D7
gaze. Sun - rise, sun - set,

Gm
Cm6
Gm
D7
Gm
Cm6
Gm
D7
sun - rise,
sun - set,
swift - ly
fly the
Gm
G7
Cm6/G
D7-9/F#
years,
One sea - son
fol - low - ing an -
Gm/F
C7/E
Cm6/E♭
D7
oth er
lad - en with
hap - pi - ness and
1
Gm
2
Gm
tears.
tears.
dim.
pp

TRY TO REMEMBER

Words by Tom Jones
Music by Harvey Schmidt

G Em7 Am7 D7 G
Try to re - mem - ber the kind of Sep - tem - ber when grass was
Try to re - mem - ber when life was so ten - der that dreams were
Deep in De - cem - ber it's nice to re - mem - ber with - out a
Em7 Am D9 Bm7
green and grain was yel - low. Try to re -
kept be - side your pil - low. Try to re -
hurt the heart is hol - low. Deep in De -
Em7 Am7 D7 Gmaj7
mem - ber the kind of Sep - tem - ber when you were a
mem - ber when life was so ten - der that love was an
cem - ber it's nice to re - mem - ber the fire of Sep -
Cmaj7 Fmaj7 D7 G
ten - der and cal - low fel - low. Try to re -
em - ber a - bout to bil - low. Try to re -
tem - ber that made us mel - low. Deep in De -

Em7 Am7 D7 1,2 G6
mem - ber and if you re - mem - ber then fol - low.
mem - ber and if you re - mem - ber then fol - low.
cem - ber our hearts should re - mem - ber and
Em7 Am7 Cmaj7/D
(echo) Fol - low, fol - low, fol - low, fol - low, fol - low, fol - low, fol - low, fol - low.
3 G6 Em7 Am7
fol - low. Fol - low, fol - low, fol - low, fol - low, fol - low,
Cmaj7/D G 6 9 Gmaj9
fol - low, fol - low, fol - low, fol - low.

GOLDEN SUNSET

WOODMAN, SPARE THAT TREE

Words by George Pope Morris
Music by Henry Russell

Additional lyrics:

When but an idle boy I sought its grateful shade
In all their gushing joy, Here, too, my sisters played;
My mother kissed me here; My father pressed my hand,
Forgive this foolish tear, But let that old oak stand.

My heart-strings round thee cling, Close as thy bark,
old friend! Here shall the wildbird sing,
And still thy branches bend. Old tree, the storm thou'lt brave,
And, woodman, leave the spot; While I've a hand to save,
Thy axe shall harm it not!

A COUNTRY WEDDING

ALL FOR LOVE

BEAUTIFUL DREAMER

Words and music by Stephen C. Foster

Bb7 Fm7 Bb7 Eb Bb7
Lulled by the moon-light have all passed a - way! Beau - ti - ful dream - er,
Eb Cm F7 Bb F7 Bb
queen of my song, List while I woo thee with soft mel - o - dy;
poco rit.
Eb Bbm/Db C7 Fm/Ab Bb Fm7 Bb7
Gone are the cares of life's bus - y throng, Beau - ti - ful dream - er a - wake un - to
a tempo
Eb Ab Eb/G Fm7 Bb7 Eb
me! Beau - ti - ful dream - er a - wake un - to me.
rall.

BILLY BOY

Moderately
mf
C
G7
Oh ___ Did she
where have you been, Bil - ly Boy, Bil - ly Boy, Oh ___
bid you come in, Bil - ly Boy, Bil - ly Boy, Did she
where have you been, charm - ing Bil - ly? ___ I have
bid you come in, charm - ing Bil - ly? ___ Yes, she

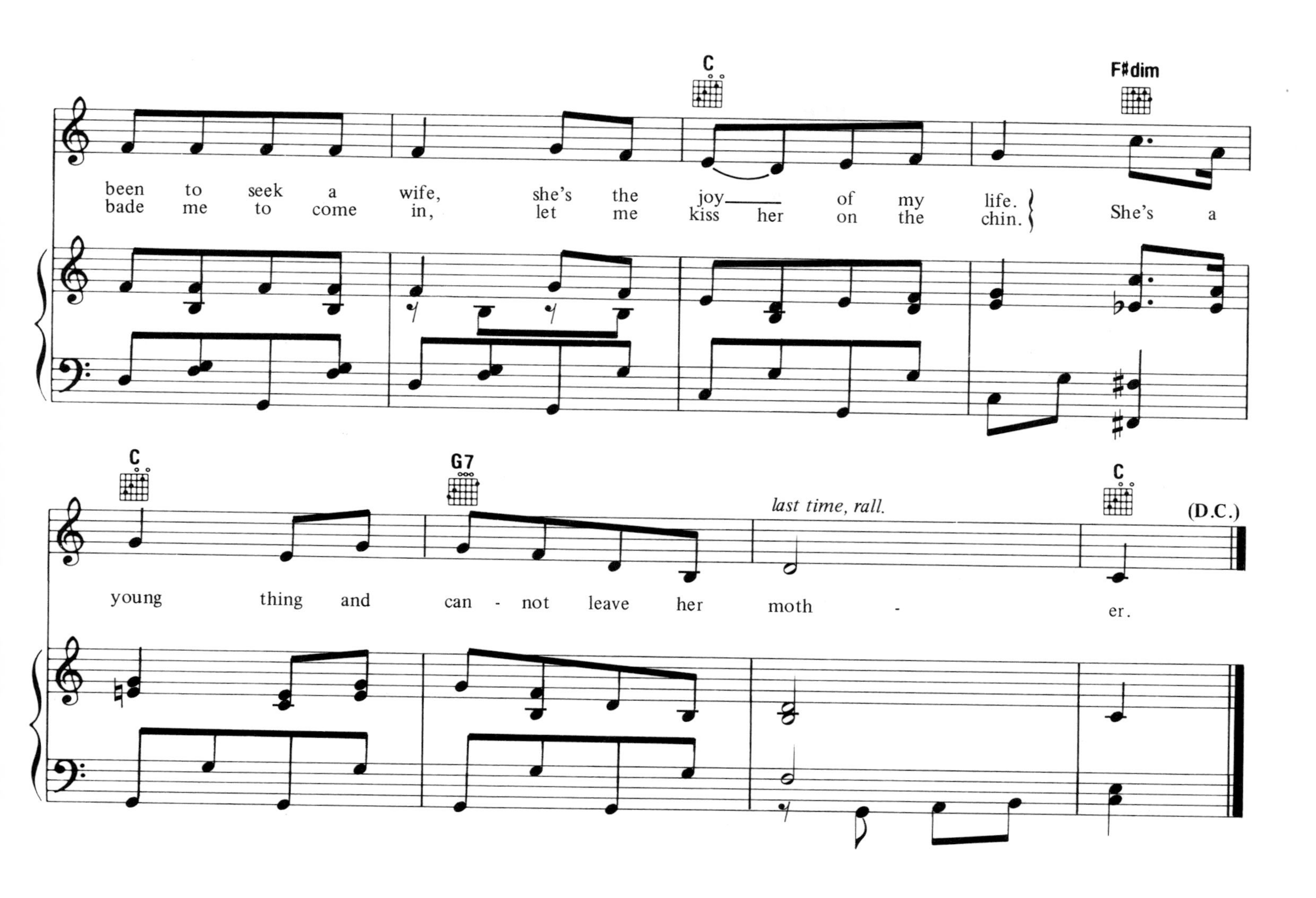

Did she set for you a chair, Billy Boy, Billy Boy,
Did she set for you a chair, charming Billy?
Yes, she set for me a chair,
And the bottom wasn't there,
She's a young thing and cannot leave her mother.

Can she bake a cherry pie, Billy Boy, Billy Boy,
Can she bake a cherry pie, charming Billy?
She can bake a cherry pie,
Quick as a cat can wink her eye,
She's a young thing and cannot leave her mother.

How old is she, Billy Boy, Billy Boy,
How old is she, charming Billy?
She's three times six and four times seven,
Twenty-eight and eleven,
She's a young thing and cannot leave her mother.

Can she sing a pretty song, Billy Boy, Billy Boy,
Can she sing a pretty song, charming Billy?
She can sing a pretty song,
But she gets the words all wrong,
She's a mother and cannot leave her young thing.

Are her eyes very bright, Billy Boy, Billy Boy,
Are her eyes very bright, charming Billy?
Yes, her eyes are very bright
But unfortunately lack sight
And she can't describe me to her mother.

CHERRY PINK AND APPLE BLOSSOM WHITE

French words by Jacques Larue
English words by Mack David
Music by Louiguy

C7
F
Eb
E♮
F
Guitar Tacet
the po - ets say.
long long a -
The sto - ry goes that once a
F
C7
go.
The boy looked in - to her eyes, it was a
F
C7
sight to en - thrall, The breez - es joined in their sighs, the blos - soms
F
C7
start - ed to fall. And as they gent - ly ca - ressed, the lov - ers

F
C7
looked up to find The branch - es of the two trees were in - ter -
F
Gm7/C
C7
twined. And that is why the po - ets al - ways write,
if there's a new moon bright a -
Fmaj7
F6
Gm7/C
bove, It's cher - ry pink and ap - ple blos - som white
C7
F
Guitar Tacet
when you're in love.

SOFT SPRING

DOWN IN THE VALLEY

Hear the wind blow, dear, hear the wind
Know I love you, dear, know I love
Bir - ming - ham Jail - house, Bir - ming - ham
D
blow,
you,
Jail,
D7
Hang your head o -
An - gels in heav -
Send it in care
ver, hear the wind
en know I love
of Bir - ming - ham
G
blow.
you.
jail.
(D.C.)

HONEYSUCKLE ROSE

Words by Andy Razaf
Music by Thomas ("Fats") Waller

C7
Bdim
C7
F#dim
Gm
G9
sweet, can't be beat, Noth - in' sweet - er ev - er stood on
Chorus - Easy Swing
Gm7/C
C7
Gm7
C7
Gm7
C7-9
feet.
Ev' - ry hon - ey bee fills with jeal - ous - y
When you're pass - ing by flow - ers droop and sigh
Gm7
Gm/C
B7/C
Am/C
B7/C
F6
G#dim
Gm7
when they see you out with me, I don't blame them, good - ness knows,
and I know the rea - son why, You're much sweet - er good - ness knows,
G#dim
F6
G#dim
Am7-5
D7-9
hon - ey - suck - le rose.
hon - ey - suck - le

2
F6 G#dim Gm7 G#dim F6 F7 Cm7/F
rose. Don't buy
Fdim F7 Bb
Guitar Tacet
sug - ar, you just have to touch my cup.
G7 Dm7/G Gdim G7 C
Guitar Tacet
You're my sug - ar, it's sweet when you
Gm7 C7
stir it up. When I'm tak - in' sips

Gm7
C7-9
Gm
Gm/E
Eb9
from your tast - y lips seems the hon - ey fair - ly
D9
Db9
C9
C9/4
F6
G#dim
Gm7
drips, You're con - fec - tion, good - ness knows,
G#dim
F6
Gm7
G#dim
F6
hon - ey - suck - le rose.
lightly
quasi Basie
8va

IN THE SHADE OF THE OLD APPLE TREE

Words by Harry W. Williams
Music by Egbert Van Alstyne

C7
F
voice that I heard like the song of a
G7
bird Seemed to whis - per sweet mu - sic to
C7
F
me. I could hear the dull
buzz of the bee In the

blos - soms as you said to me,
C7
"With a heart that is true, I'll be
F7
B♭
D♭7
F/C
C♯dim
G7
C7
wait - ing for you In the shade of the old ap - ple
1
F6
F♯dim
C7
tree." In the
2
F
tree."
rit.

APPLE PICKERS

I TALK TO THE TREES

Words by Alan Jay Lerner
Music by Frederick Loewe

Gm7/C
Gm
C7
C7-9
F6/9
I talk to them all in vain.
Bb
Bdim
But sud-den-ly my words reach some-one
mf
Fmaj7/C
F
F#dim
Gm
Gm(+7)
Gm7
G9
el-se's ear, Touch some-one el-se's heart-strings,
Db9+11
C9
Guitar Tacet
Gm7
too. I tell you my dreams,

C7-9
Fmaj7
Gm7/C
And while you're list - 'ning to me,
I sud - den - ly
Gm7
C7
C7-9
F6/9
see them come true.
To Interlude
F6/9
Fine
I can see us on an
true.
Interlude
C7
F
A - pril night,
look - in' out a - cross a
roll - in' farm,

C7
Hav - in' sup - per in the can - dle - light, walk - in' la - ter arm in
sim.
F6
C7
arm. Then I'll tell you how I passed the day,
F
think - in' main - ly how the night would be, And I'll try to find the
C7
C
G7
C7
F
D.C. al Fine
words to say all the things you mean to me.

LAZY AFTERNOON

Words by John Latouche
Music by Jerome Moross

D7
Dm7
D9
It's a la - zy af - ter - noon And the
Dm9
G7
Dm7
farm - er leaves his reap - in', In the mea - dow cows are sleep - in' And the speck - led trout stop leap - in' up -
G7
Dm7
G9
Dm7
stream as we dream. A fat pink cloud hangs
very smoothly
G7
Cmaj7
C6
Dm7
o - ver the hill, un - fold - in' like a rose. If you hold my hand and

G7
C6
Dm7
Em7
sit real still You can hear the grass as it grows. It's a
Am7
A9
Am7
ha - zy af - ter - noon And I know a place that's qui - et 'cept for
D7
Am7
D7
dais - ies run - ning ri - ot And there's no one pass - ing by it to see. Come
Am7
D7
A6
spend this la - zy af - ter - noon with me.

WILLIAMSTOWN

LET IT SNOW! LET IT SNOW! LET IT SNOW!

Words by Sammy Cahn
Music by Jule Styne

C7
F
F/A
Abdim
does-n't show signs of stop - ping, and I brought some corn for
C7/G
D7/A
Bbmaj7
Am7-5
Gm7
F#dim
Gm7
G13
pop - ping. The lights are turned way down low, Let it
C7
F
C
snow! Let it snow! Let it snow! When we fin - al - ly kiss good -
C#dim
Dm7
G7
C6
night, how I'll hate go - ing out in the storm. But if

D9
G7
you'll real - ly hold me tight, all the way home I'll be
Gm7/C
Am7
D7+5 -9
G9
C7-9
F
Bb9
warm. The fire is slow - ly dy - ing, and my
F/A
Abdim
C7/G
D7/A
Bbmaj7
Am7
Gm7
F#dim
dear, we're still good - bye - ing, But as long as you love me
Gm7
Bdim
C7
F
so, Let it snow! Let it snow! Let it snow!
8 bassa

IT SNOWS, OH IT SNOWS

OH! DEAR, WHAT CAN THE MATTER BE?

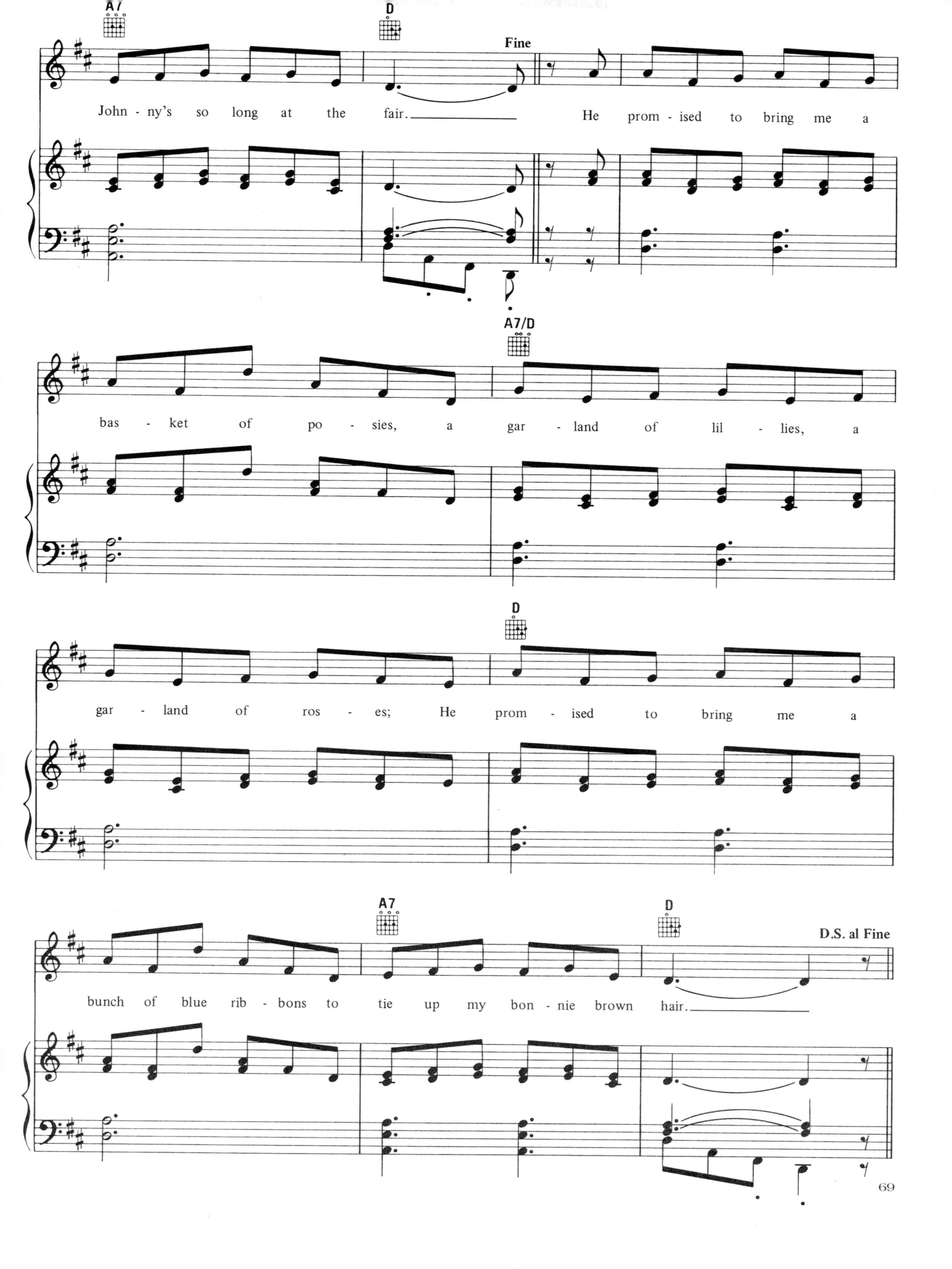

A7
D
Fine
Johnny's so long at the fair.
He promised to bring me a
A7/D
basket of posies, a garland of lilies, a
D
garland of roses; He promised to bring me a
A7
D
D.S. al Fine
bunch of blue ribbons to tie up my bonnie brown hair.

SEPTEMBER SONG

Words by Maxwell Anderson
Music by Kurt Weill

Am7 Am6 G7/4 G#dim Am7 Am6
Guitar Tacet
lieu of pearls. And as time came a-round, she came my way, As
songs they sing, And a plen-ti-ful waste of time of day, A
Dm7 Dbmaj7 Cmaj7 Cm6
in tempo
time came a-round she came.
plen-ti-ful waste of time.
Oh, it's a long long while
Cm-6 C Cmaj7 C7 D7
from May to De-cem-ber,
But the days grow short
Fm6 C Cm6
when you reach Sep-tem-ber.
When the au-tumn weath-er

Cm-6
C(add9)
Cmaj7
C7
turns the leaves to flame,
One has - n't got
D7
Fm6
Cmaj7
time
for the wait - ing game.
Fm
Oh, the days dwin - dle down
to a
F#dim
Fm
pre - cious few!
Sep - tem - ber,
No -

F♯dim
Guitar Tacet
Cm6
vem - ber!
L.H.
And these few pre - cious days
calmly
Cm-6
C
Cmaj7
C7
I'll spend with you,
These pre - cious
D7
Fm
1
C
Fm
days I'll spend with you.
When you
2
C
Dm7-5
C
you.
rall.

SOON IT'S GONNA RAIN

Words by Tom Jones
Music by Harvey Schmidt

C6
C6
do?
you?
We'll
Dm7/G
G7
G7+5
Cmaj7
find four limbs of a tree. We'll build four
G
Am7/G
F/G
C/F
Bm7-5
E7
walls and a floor. We'll bind it o - ver with leaves, then
Am7
D9
Ab7
G7-9
Cmaj9
C6
duck in - side to stay. Then we'll let it rain;

Cmaj9
C6
Cmaj9
C6
Cmaj9
A7
We'll not feel it. Then we'll let it rain, rain pell mell.
Am7
Dm7
G9
G7-9
Em7/A
And we'll not com - plain if it nev - er stops at all,
A7-9 -5
Dm7
Em7
Fmaj7
G7 4
G7-9
We'll live and love with - in our own four
C6
walls.

A STORM IS ON THE WATERS NOW

WAITING FOR SANTA CLAUS

TELL ME WHY

Moderately
G
C#dim
D7
B7
C
G/B
D#dim
Em
Em7
A7
A9-5
B♭dim
Am/C
E7
1. Please tell me why the stars do shine,
2. Be - cause God made the stars to shine, Be -
3. I know it's true that God a - bove, He
Tell me why the i - vy twines, Then tell me why the
cause God made the i - vy twine, Be - cause God made the
want - ed some - one for me to love, And He chose you from
sky is blue, And I will tell you why I love you.
sky so blue, Be - cause God made you so sweet and true.
all the rest Be - cause He knew, dear, I'd love you the best.
D.C.

SWEET GENEVIEVE

Words by George Cooper
Music by Henry Tucker

G
D7
G
ev - 'ry dream my wak - ing thoughts are full of thee; Thy
no re - gret what - e'er the years may bring to me; I
B7
Em
B7
Em
Am
Em
C7
B
D7
glance is in the star - ry beam that falls a - long the sum - mer sea.
bless the hour when we first met, the hour that gave me love and thee. Oh
G
D7
G
3
Gen - e - vieve, sweet Gen - e - vieve, the days may come the days may go. But
C
G/D
D7
Cm6/G
G
D.C.
still the hands of mem - 'ry weave the bliss - ful dreams of long a - go.

WAIT FOR THE WAGON

Words and music R.B. Buckley

G7
C
morn - ing when I am by your side, We'll
sto - ry, it will re - lieve my heart, So
F
G7
C
jump in - to the wag - on and all take a ride.
jump in - to the wag - on and off we will start.
C
C7
F
f
Wait for the wag - on, wait for the wag - on,
C
F
G7
C
(D.C.)
Wait for the wag - on and we'll all take a ride.

WHEN THE CORN IS WAVING, ANNIE DEAR

Words and music by Charles Blamphin

Eb F7 Bb Fine Bb7 Eb Ebm
greet thy win - ning smile. The moon will be at
both our hearts know well. Where wild flow'rs in their
Bb Bb7 Eb Ebm Bb D7 G7
full, love, the stars will bright - ly gleam. Oh
beau - ty will scent the eve - ning breeze, Oh
C7 F Bdim F/C C7
come, my queen of night, love, And grace the beau - teous
haste, the stars are peep - ing, And the moon's be - hind the
1 F F7 2 F F7 D.S. al Fine
scene. When the trees. When the

THE WORLD IS WAITING FOR THE SUNRISE

Words by Eugene Lockhart
Music by Ernest Seitz

Fm6/G
G7
G+
C6
G+
C6
dew. The thrush on high
G+
C6
E7
his sleep - y mate is call - ing
F6
F#dim
C
B+
Gm/Bb
A7
Fm6/Ab
and my heart is call -
G7
G+
C
Ab7
Dm7
Bb7
G7
Dm7
G9
G7+5
C6
- ing you.

Moses.

THE BIRDS AND THE BEASTS WERE THERE

RUN PIG RUN

ANIMAL FAIR

Brightly, in 2 (♩. = 1 beat)
I
f dim.
mp
C
went to the an - i - mal fair, the birds and the beasts were
G7
there. The big ba - boon by the light of the moon was

C
C(add9)
comb - ing his au - burn hair. You ought to have seen the
monk, he jumped on the el - e - phant's trunk. The el - e - phant sneezed and
Em7
Fmaj7
fell on his knees, and what be - came of the monk, the monk, the monk, the monk, the
G7
Repeat ad lib
Guitar Tacet
p sub.
monk? The monk?

THE BARNYARD SONG

Additional lyrics:

I had a pig and the pig pleased me.
I fed my pig on a green berry tree.
The little pig went "oink oink"
Chorus:

I had a cow and the cow pleased me.
I fed my cow on a green berry tree.
The little cow went "moo moo"
Chorus:

I had a baby and the baby pleased me.
I fed my baby on a green berry tree.
The little baby went "waah waah"
Chorus:

BAA! BAA! BLACK SHEEP

BONDSVILLE FAIR

TAKING IN LAUNDRY

EENSY WEENSY SPIDER

THE GLOW WORM

Modern version by Johnny Mercer
Original lyric by Lilla Cayley Robinson
Music by Paul Lincke

Dm7 G7 C
Turn on the A C and the D C. This night could use a
Il - lu - mi - nate yon woods pri - me - val. See how the shad - ows
Which you can make both slow or "faz - da." I don't know who you
Dm7 G7
lit - tle bright - nin', Light up, you l'il ol'
deep and dark - en, you and your chick should
took a shine to Or who you're out to
C
bug of light - nin'. When you got - ta glow, you
get to spark - in'. I got a gal that
make a sign to. I got a gal that
D7 1,2 G7/4 Dm7/G Cdim/G C
got - ta glow, glow, lit - tle glow - worm, glow!
I love so, glow, lit - tle glow - worm, glow!
I love so,

Original words
Shine, little glowworm, glimmer, glimmer,
Shine, little glowworm, glimmer, glimmer.
Lead us, lest too far we wander,
Love's sweet voice is calling yonder!
Shine, little glowworm, glimmer, glimmer,
Shine, little glowworm, glimmer, glimmer!
Light the path, below, above
And lead us on to Love!

A BEAUTIFUL WORLD

THE FOX

Brightly, with humor
D
A7
D7
G
D
A7
D
mp – mf
The fox went out in the chill - y night, He
ran till he came to a great big bin, The
prayed for the moon to give him light; He'd man - y a mile to
ducks and the geese were kept there - in; A cou - ple of you will
go that night be - fore he reached the town - o,
grease my chin be - fore I leave this town - o,

3. So he grabbed a gray goose by the neck
And threw a duck across his back;
He didn't mind their "quack, quack, quack"
And their legs all dangling down-o, down-o, down-o,
He didn't mind their "quack, quack, quack"
And their legs all dangling down-o.

4. Then old Mother Flipper-flopper jumped out of bed
And out of the window she stuck her head;
Said, "John, John, the gray goose is gone,
And the fox is in the town-o, town-o, town-o" etc.

5. So John he ran to the top of the hill
And he blew his horn both loud and shrill;
The fox he said, "I better flee with my kill
Or they'll soon be on my trail-o, trail-o, trail-o," etc.

6. He ran till he came to his cozy den
And there were his little ones, eight, nine, and ten;
They said, "Daddy, you better go back again
'Cause it must be a mighty fine town-o, town-o, town-o," etc.

7. So the fox and his wife, without any strife,
They cut up the goose with a fork and a knife;
They never had such a supper in their lives
And the little ones chewed on the bones-o, bones-o, bones-o, etc.

MY OLD HEN

With rollicking good humor
G D7 G D7 G
My old hen's a good old hen, she lays eggs for the farm-er men; Some-times
mf
D7 G D7 G D7 G
one, some-times two, some-times 'nough for the whole darn crew! Cluck, old hen, cluck, I tell; You cluck, old
C G D7 G D7 G C D7 G
hen, or I'm a-goin' to sell you. Cluck, old hen, cluck, I say, cluck, old hen, I'll give you a-way.

IN THE SPRINGTIME

OH WHERE, OH WHERE HAS MY LITTLE DOG GONE?

Words by Septimus Winner

CANDLE DIP DAY IN 1800

OLD DOG TRAY

Words and music by Stephen C. Foster

D/C
B
Am
G/D
D7
G
on the vil - lage green, a — sport - ing with my old dog Tray.
D
D7
G
D
D7
Old dog Tray's ev - er faith - ful, grief can - not drive him a -
B/D#
D7
G
D7/F#
way, He's gen - tle, he is kind, I shall
D7
B7
Am
G/D
D7
G
nev - er, nev - er find a bet - ter friend than old dog Tray.

THE OLE GREY GOOSE

EARLY SPRINGTIME ON THE FARM

ROBIN REDBREAST

F7
Bb
thrush - es now are si - lent, our swal - lows flown a - way, But
leath - r'y pears and ap - ples hang rus - set on the bough, 'Tis
frost - y ways, like i - ron, the branch - es plum'd with snow, A -
Rob - bin's here in coat of brown and scar - let breast - knot gay.
au - tumn, au - tumn, au - tumn late, 'Twill soon be win - ter now.
las! in win - ter dead and dark, Where can poor Rob - in go?
Oh
Rob - in, Rob - in Red - breast, Oh Rob - in, Rob - in, dear, Oh Rob - in sings so
mf
Gm
Eb
C/E
Bb/F
sweet - ly in the fall - ing of the year.
p
(D.C.)

THE SOW TOOK THE MEASLES

3. What do you think I made of her tail?
 The very best whup that ever sought sail.
 Whup or whup socket, any such thing,
 The sow took the measles and she died in the spring.

4. What do you think I made of her feet?
 The very best pickles that you ever did eat.
 Pickles or glue or any such thing,
 The sow took the measles and she died in the spring.

UPWARD AND ONWARD

BLACK HORSES

APRIL SHOWERS

Words by B.G. DeSylva
Music by Louis Silvers

D/A
A7
Guitar Tacet
Eb9
D9
here's the point that you should nev - er miss: Though A - pril
Chorus
With an easy swing
Am7
Am7/D D7
Gmaj9
G6
Am7
show - ers may come your way, they bring the flow - ers
Am7/D D7
G6/9
Gmaj7 Am7 Bm7
E7
that bloom in May; So if it's rain - ing have no re -
Am
C#m7-5
grets, be - cause it is - n't rain - ing rain, you know, it's

D7 C#7 Am G#dim D7 Am7 Am7/D D7
rain - ing vi - o - lets. And where you see clouds up - on the
Gmaj9 G6 B7-5 E7
hills, you soon will see crowds of daf - fo -
Am7 Am7-5 Gmaj7+5 Em7
dils. So keep on look - ing for a blue - bird and lis - t'ning for his
A7sus A7 Am7 Bb9-5 Am7 Am7/D D13-9 G6
Guitar Tacet
song when - ev - er A - pril show - ers come a - long.
8va

THE THUNDERSTORM

THE BEST THINGS IN LIFE ARE FREE

Music and Lyrics by B.G. DeSylva, Lew Brown, and Ray Henderson

Dm7
stars be - long to ev' - ry - one, they
G7 Dm7 G7+5 -9 Cmaj9 C6 Cmaj9 C6
gleam there for you and me. The
C9 Gm7 F#dim C7 Gb7 F6 E7 Fmaj7 E9 Eb9-5
flow - ers in spring, the rob - ins that sing, The
D9 Am7 G#dim D9 Dm7 G13 G7+5
sun - beams that shine, They're yours! They're mine! And

C
F#m7-5
B7-5
E7
Eb7-5
love can come to ev' - ry - one, the
D13
Fm/G
G7-9
1
C6
Eb9
Ab7
G7+5+9
best things in life are free. The
2
C6
Eb9
D9
Db9
C6 9
free.

THE FAMILY PICNIC

CLIMB EV'RY MOUNTAIN

Words by Oscar Hammerstein II
Music by Richard Rodgers

C D/C G/B Gm/B♭ Fmaj7/A
Climb ev' - ry moun - tain, ford ev' - ry stream,
mp
Fm/A♭ C/G Dm7 G7 C
Fol - low ev' - ry rain - bow, till you find your dream! A
F Dm7 G7 G/F C/E
dream that will need all the love you can give
cresc. poco a poco
D7 G Em7 A7 A/G
Ev' - ry day of your life for as long as you

D/F♯
G
A/G
live.
Climb ev' - ry
cresc. molto
ff
D/F♯
Dm/F
G/F
Cmaj7/E
moun - tain, ford ev' - ry stream,
Am
Em/G
Dm7
C/G
C+/G
Fol - low ev - 'ry rain - bow till you
p
cresc.
ff
Dm7/G
G7
C
find your dream!

HOOSICK RIVER, SUMMER

RAINBOW

LOOK TO THE RAINBOW

Words by E.Y. Harburg
Music by Burton Lane

Moderately and rather freely

A Asus A
lips and a song for your heart To sing it when -
old, and you nev - er stand still With whip - poor wills
earth, and I scanned all the skies, But I found it at
Flowing forward in strict time
A7 G D(no3rd) D
ev - er the world falls a - part." "Look,
sing - in' be - yond the next hill.
last in my own true love's eyes.
mf
Bm Em7 A7 D Em7 A7
look, look to the rain - bow, fol - low it
D G Bm6 A7 4 A7 D
o - ver the hill and stream, Look,

Bm
Em7
A7
D
G
look, look to the rain - bow, fol - low the
D/A
A7/4
A7
1.2.
D
Guitar Tacet
3.
D
fel - low who fol - lows a dream." 'twas a dream."
So I
Freely and sustained
G
D/F♯
Em7
D
Fol - low the fel - low, fol - low the fel - low,
G
D/A
A7/4
A7
D
fol - low the fel - low who fol - lows a dream.
rall.

MY FAVORITE THINGS

Words by Oscar Hammerstein II
Music by Richard Rodgers

Am7
D7
Bm7
C/E
Brown pa - per pack - ag - es tied up with strings,
Wild geese that fly with the moon on their wings,
G
C
F♯m7-5
B7
These are a few of my fa - vor - ite things.
1
Em
2
E(major)
mf
E
Girls in white dress - es with blue sat - in sash - es;

A
Snow - flakes that stay on my nose and eye - lash - es;
Am7
D7
Bm7
C/E
Sil - ver white win - ters that melt in - to springs;
G
C
F♯m7-5
B7+5-9
These are a few of my fa - vor - ite things.
Em
F♯m7-5
B7
When the dog bites, When the bee stings,

Em
Em/D
Em/C#
Cmaj7
When I'm feel - ing sad, I
A7
sim - ply re - mem - ber my fa - vor - ite things, And
G/D
C/D
D7+5 -9
D7 6
then I don't feel so
G
(Guitar Tacet)
bad.
lightly

MY GRANDMA'S ADVICE

Words and music by "M"

3. The first came a-courting was little Johny Green,
As fine a young man as ever was seen;
But the words of my Grandma run in my head,
And I could not hear one word he said.
Tim-e-i tim-e um tum tim-e um pa ta
And I could not hear one word he said.

4. The next came a courting was young Ellis Grove,
'Twas then we met with a joyous love;
With a joyous love I couldn't be afraid,
You'd better get married than die an old maid.
Tim-e-i tim-e um tum tim-e um pa ta
You'd better get married than die an old maid.

5. Think I to myself there's some mistake,
What a fuss these old folks make;
If the boys and the girls had all been so afraid,
Then Grandma herself would have died an old maid.
Tim-e-i tim-e um tum tim-e um pa ta
Then Grandma herself would have died an old maid.

OH, WHAT A BEAUTIFUL MORNIN'

Words by Oscar Hammerstein II
Music by Richard Rodgers

C
G7
mead - ow. The corn is as high as an
stat - ues, They don't turn their heads as they
mu - sic, The breeze is so bus - y it
C
Fmaj7
Em7
Ebmaj7
el - e - phant's eye An' it looks like it's climb - in' clear
see me ride by But a lit - tle brown mav - 'rick is
don't miss a tree And a ol' weep - in' wil - ler is
Dm7
Db9
Chorus, in strict time
C
up to the sky.
wink - in' her eye.
laugh - in' at me.
Oh, what a beau - ti - ful
rall.
Bb/F
F
C
C/B
morn - in'! Oh, what a beau - ti - ful

D7/A
G7
C
day!
I got a beau - ti - ful
F
F#dim
C/G
G7
feel - in'
ev - 'ry - thing's go - in' my
1,2
C
Guitar Tacet
way.
2. All the
3. All the
3
C
Dm
G7
way,
C/G
G7
C
Oh, what a beau - ti - ful day.
rall.
delicately

A BEAUTIFUL MORNING

ON A CLEAR DAY (YOU CAN SEE FOREVER)

Words by Alan Jay Lerner
Music by Burton Lane

C#7 D7 Bm7 Bdim G6 B♭dim Am7 G#dim
that the glow of your be - ing out - shines ev' - ry
Am7 D7 Dm7/G
star. You feel part of ev' - ry
G9+5 Cmaj7 Gm/B♭
moun - tain, sea and shore. You can hear from far and
A7 4 E♭7-5 D9 Am7 D7
Guitar Tacet
near a world you've nev - er heard be - fore. And on a

C#dim/G
Gmaj7
F9+11
E9 4
E7
clear day, on that clear day
Am7
Bm7
C
Bm
You can see for - ev - er and
ev - er and ev - er and ev -
D7-9
G6
Guitar Tacet
F#7+5 +9
er - more!

HOOSICK VALLEY (FROM THE WINDOW)

SUGARING OFF

YOUNG AT HEART

Words by Carolyn Leigh
Music by Johnny Richards

Dm7-5 G7 Dm7-5 G7 G+ C9/4 C7
go to ex - tremes with im - pos - si - ble schemes, you can laugh when your dreams fall a -
C9/4 C7 C7-9 F7 Bdim F7 Bdim F7 Cm7 F7 F+
part at the seams and life gets more ex - cit - ing with each pass - ing day, and
Bb6 A6/Bb Bb6 A6/Bb Cm7 F+ Bb
love is eith - er in your heart or on the way. Don't you know that it's worth ev'ry
Dbdim Cm Cm(+7) Cm7 Cm6
trea - sure on earth to be young at heart? For as

F7 Cm7 F7 F+ B♭ E♭maj9
rich as you are, it's much bet-ter by far to be young at heart.
B♭ E♭maj9 Dm7-5 G7 Dm7-5 G7
And if you should sur-vive to a hun-dred and five, look at
C9/4 C7 E♭maj7 E♭m B♭/F
all you'll de-rive out of be-ing a-live! And here is the best part,
F7 B♭6 B♭7/6 Cm7/B♭ Edim/B♭ Cm7 C♯dim B♭6
you have a head start if you are a-mong the ver-y young at heart.

THERE'S MUSIC IN THE AIR

Words by Fanny Crosby
Music by George F. Root

D7
G
on the bright and laugh - ing sky.
on the dis - tant moun - tain stream.
as its pen - sive beau - ties die.
C
C#dim
G
D7
Many a harp's ec - stat - ic sound with its thrill of
When be - neath some grate - ful shade sor - row's ach - ing
Then, oh then, the loved one's gone wake the pure ce -
G/B
C
C#dim
joy pro - found While we list en -
head is laid Sweet - ly to the
les - tial song, An - gel voic - es
G
Em7
A7
D7
G
(D.C.)
chant - ed there to the mu - sic in the air.
spir - it there comes the mu - sic in the air.
greet us there in the mu - sic in the air.

SUDDENLY THERE'S A VALLEY

Words and music by Chuck Meyer and Biff Jones

Fm6
C
G7
C
F
peace with man. When a
nev - er
end.
C
F
Dm6
C/E
C7
Touched on - ly by the sea - sons, Swept
F
Fm
C
Am
clean by the wav - ing grain, Sur - veyed by a
Am/G♯
Am/G
Am/F♯
Am
F♯m7-5
hap - py blue - bird And kissed by the fall - ing

Fm6
G7
C
Fm
rain. When you think there's no bright to-
mor-rows And you feel you can't try a-
C7
F
gain, Sud-den-ly there's a val-ley
Fmaj7
F♯dim
Where hope and love be-gin.
rall.

MISSOURI

THE SOUND OF MUSIC

Words by Oscar Hammerstein II
Music by Richard Rodgers

E/F
F/A
Gm7
with the sound of mu - sic;
My heart wants to sing ev'-ry
C7
Gm7/C
F6
Gm7
G♯dim
Am
B♭
Gdim
song it hears.
My heart wants to beat like the wings of the
F/A
F
B♭
Gdim
F/A
B♭
Gdim
birds that rise from the lake to the trees.
My heart wants to sigh like a
F/A
Dm7
G7/4
G7
G7-5
C7/4
C7
F
chime that flies from a church on a breeze,
To

Bb
Gdim
F/A
F
Bb
Gdim
laugh like a brook when it trips and falls o - ver stones on its
F/A
Dm
Bm7-5
Am
way, To sing through the night like a
Dm7
G7
C7
Gb7-5
F6/9
lark who is learn - ing to pray. I go to the hills
E/F
when my heart is lone - ly, I

F6/9
Bb/F
know I will hear what I've heard be - fore.
Bbm/F
Db7
F
Am/E
F7/Eb
My heart will be blessed with the sounds of
Bb/D
Bbm/Db
Am/C
mu - sic And I'll sing
C7
F6/9
once more.
dim. e rall.

CATCHING THE TURKEY

BUT ONCE A YEAR

I'LL BE HOME ON CHRISTMAS DAY

Words and music by Michael Jarrett

F
F7
see. But if I could on-ly bor-row One
B♭
C7
dream from yes-ter-day, I'd be on that train to-
mor-row, I'd be home on
F
Christ-mas Day.
F
F7
B♭
Been so man-y times be-fore, she left that can-dle burn-ing, And
time I think a-bout her, all the love I left be-hind,

C7
oh, too many tears that fell, My soul filled with
mem - o - ries still lin - ger With - in my trou - bled
F
F7
yearn - ing. If I had an - y sense at all, I'd
mind. If I could set a - side my pride And
B♭
C7
just be on my way. I'd be on that train to - mor - row, And be
I'd be on my way. I'd catch that train to - mor - row, And be
1
F
2
F
B♭
F
home on Christ-mas Day. Ev' - ry Day.

CHRISTMAS AT HOME

O TANNENBAUM

Gm C7 F Bb F
sym - bol of e - ter - ni - ty. Your boughs are green through -
treu sind dei - ne Blät - ter. Du grünst nicht nur zur
mf
Gm C7 F F C
out the year, re - splend - ent in a life sin - cere. O Christ - mas Tree, O
Som - mer - zeit, mein auch im Win - ter wenn es schneit. O Tan - nen - baum, O
f
F Gm C7 1 F 2 F
Christ - mas Tree, true sym - bol of e - ter - ni - ty. O Blät - ter.
Tan - nen - baum, wie treu sind dei - ne
Dm C F Cm6 D7 Gm C7 F
poco maestoso

ON THE FIRST THANKSGIVING DAY

THANKSGIVING

OVER THE RIVER AND THROUGH THE WOODS

OVER THE RIVER

THE SLEIGHING GLEE

Words and music by T.J. Cook

C
G7
C
Swift - ly o'er the snow we go, moon - beams spar - kle 'round;
Glide a - long with laugh and song o'er the fleec - y snow;
G7
C7
Hoofs keep time to mu - sic's chime, mer - ri - ly on we bound.
Swift - ly ride with friend be - side, cheer - i - ly on we go.
A -
F
C7
F
way, a - way, a - way we go, mer - ri - ly o'er the fleec - y snow. A -
C7
F
way, a - way, a - way we go mer - ri - ly on we bound.

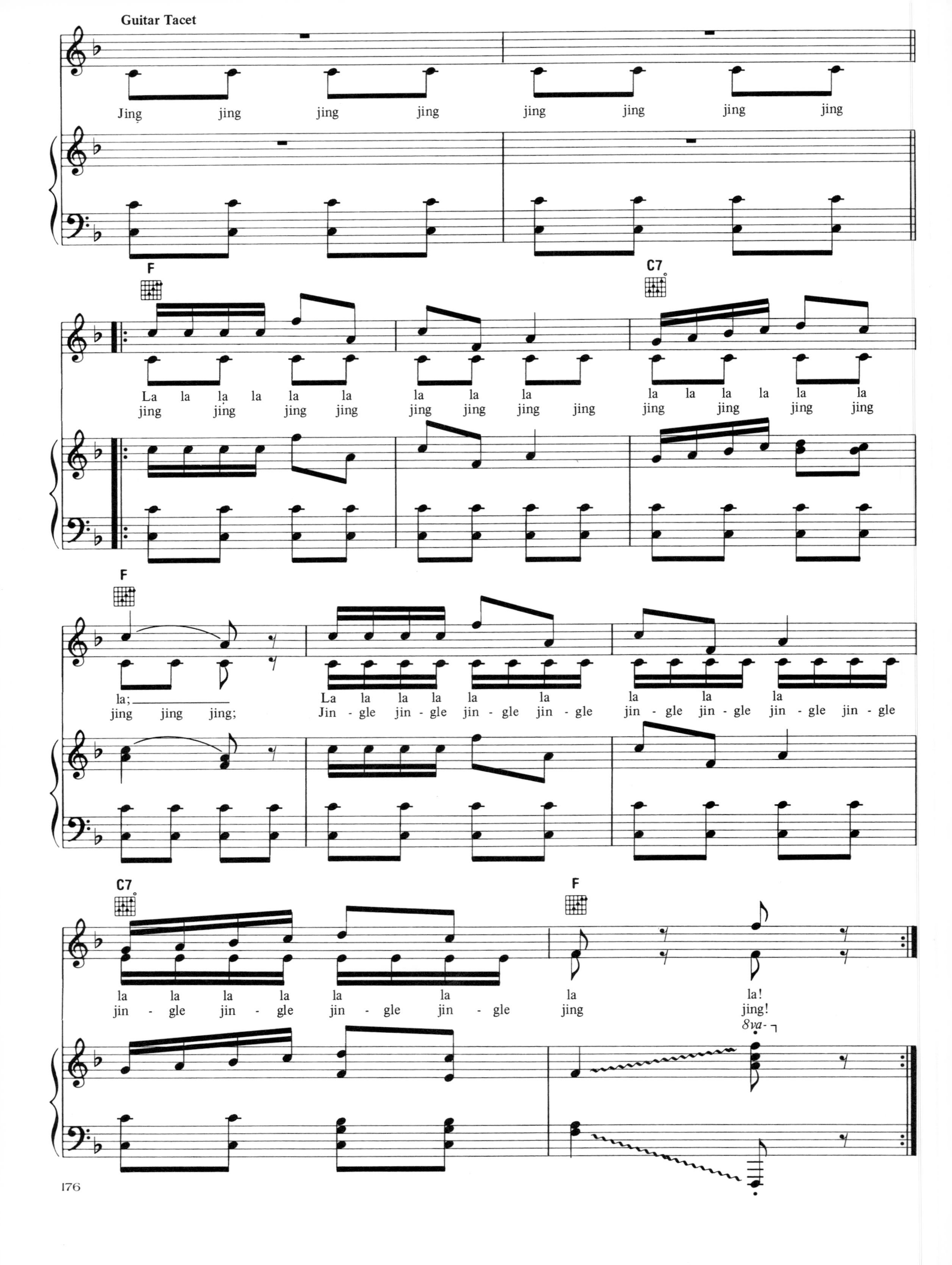
Guitar Tacet
Jing jing jing jing jing jing jing jing
F
C7
La la la la la la la la la la la la la la la
jing jing jing jing jing jing jing jing jing jing jing jing
F
la; La la la la la la la la la
jing jing jing; Jin - gle jin - gle jin - gle jin - gle jin - gle jin - gle jin - gle jin - gle
C7
F
la la la la la la la la!
jin - gle jin - gle jin - gle jin - gle jing jing!
8va

JOY RIDE

OF THEE I SING

THE FLAG

AMERICA THE BEAUTIFUL

Music by Samuel A. Ward
Words by Katherine Lee Bates

2. O beautiful for pilgrim feet,
Whose stern impassioned stress,
A thoroughfare for freedom beat
Across the wilderness.
America! America!
God mend thine ev'ry flaw,
Confirm thy soul in self-control,
Thy liberty in law.

3. O beautiful for patriot dream
That sees beyond the years,
Thine alabaster cities gleam,
Undimmed by human tears.
America! America!
God shed His grace on thee,
And crown thy good with brotherhood
From sea to shining sea.

COLUMBIA, THE GEM OF THE OCEAN

Words and music by David T. Shaw

D
G
G/B
C
view. Thy ban - ners make ty - ran - ny trem - ble When
f
Am
D
D7
G
D
borne by the red, white, and blue, When borne by the red, white, and
(f)
G
D
G
G/B
blue, When borne by the red, white, and blue, Thy ban - ners make ty - ran - ny
mp
cresc.
C
Am
D
D7
G
Maestoso
trem - ble When borne by the red, white, and blue!
f

THE HOUSE I LIVE IN

Words by Lewis Allan
Music by Earl Robinson

A7/4 A7 A7 D A/C♯ D
me? The house I live in, a plot of earth, a street, The
The place I work in, the work-er at my side, The
G6 D/F♯ F D A/G D/F♯
groc-er and the butch-er and the peo-ple that I meet, The chil-dren in the play-ground, the
lit-tle town or cit-y where my peo-ple lived and died, The "how-dy" and the hand-shake, the
A7/C♯ Bm G D/F♯ Em7 A7 D
fac-es that I see, All rac-es, all re-lig-ions, that's A-mer-i-ca to me.
air of feel-ing free, The right to speak my mind out, that's A-mer-i-ca to me.
G D/F♯ Em7 A7 D Em7 A7 D
The

C F# D C F# D
things I see a - bout me, the big things and the small, The
D/C G/B D/F# G
lit - tle cor - ner news - stand, and the house a mile tall, The
Em Bm F#/A# Bm A/E
wed - ding and the church-yard, the laugh - ter and the tears, The dream that's been a - grow - in' for a
E7 A A7 D A/C# D
hun - dred fif - ty years. The town I live in, the street, the house, the room, The

G6 D/F# F D
pave - ment of the cit - y or a gar - den all in bloom, The
A/G D/F# A7/C# Bm
church, the school, the club house, The mil - lion lights I see, but es -
G D/A G/A A7 Em7/A
pec - ial - ly the peo - ple, that's A - mer - i - ca to
D G D/A G/A A7 D
me!
rall.
8va

OUR STATE FAIR

Words by Oscar Hammerstein II
Music by Richard Rodgers

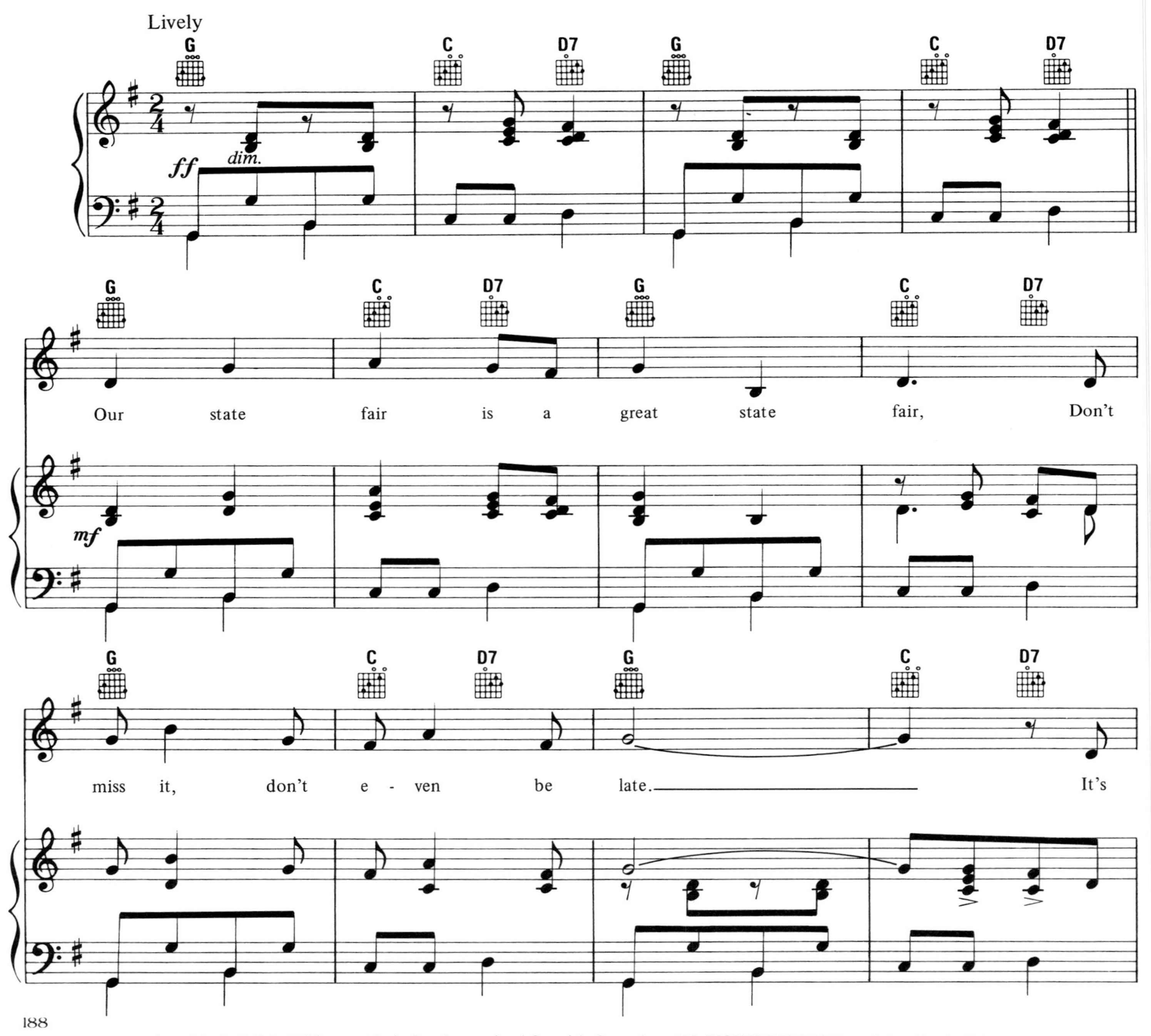

G
C
D7
G
C
D7
dol - lars to dough - nuts that our state fair is the
G
C
D7
1.
G
C
D7
(D.C.)
best state fair in our state!
2.
G
C
D7
G
C
D7
state!
G6
accel.
R.H.
L.H.
R.H.

SHENANDOAH

Slowly
F
Dm
F
Dm
B♭
Gm
Oh, Shen - an - doah, I long to hear you,
Oh, Shen - an - doah, I love your daugh-ter,
Oh, Shen - an - doah, I'm bound to leave you,
A - way you roll - ing
mp
quasi harp
F
Am
Dm
Am/C
B♭
F/A
riv - er.
Oh, Shen - an - doah I long to hear you.
For her I'd cross your roam - ing wat - er.
Oh, Shen - an - doah I'll not de - ceive you.
A
Dm
B♭
F/A
B♭
F/C
Dm
C
F
B♭/F
F
(D.C.)
way, I'm bound a - way, 'Cross the wide Mis - sou - ri.

SHENANDOAH

STARS AND STRIPES FOREVER

Music by John Philip Sousa

C
F
G
ff
C
grandioso
E7
Am
Fm/Ab
Ab
C/G
G7
C
ff

A LITTLE WORK

OUR BARN

THE FARMER'S IN THE DELL

3. The wife takes a nurse, etc.

4. The nurse takes a child, etc.

5. The child takes a dog, etc.

6. The dog takes a cat, etc.

7. The cat takes a rat, etc.

8. The rat takes the cheese, etc.

9. The cheese stands alone, etc.

HOME FOR THANKSGIVING

THE HONEST PLOUGHMAN

3. The rent that time was not so high, but far as I will pen,
For now one family's nearly twice as big as then was ten;
When I was born my father used to harrow, plough, and sow,
I think I've heard my mother say, 'twas ninety years ago.

4. To drive the plough, my father did a boy engage,
Until that I had just arrived to seven years of age;
So then he did no servant want, my mother milked the cow,
And with the lark I rose each morn to go and drive the plough.

5. When I was fifteen years of age, I used to thrash and sow,
I harrowed, ploughed, and harvest-time I used to reap and mow;
When I was twenty years of age, I could manage well the farm,
I could hedge and ditch, and plough and sow, or thrash within the barn.

6. At length when I was twenty-five, I took myself a wife,
Compelled to leave my father's house, as I have changed my life;
The younger children in my place, my father's work would do,
Then daily as an husbandman to labour I did go.

7. My wife and me, tho' very poor, could keep a pig and cow,
She could sit and knit, and spin, and I the land could plough;
There nothing was upon a farm at all, but I could do,
I feel things very different now - that's many years ago.

8. We lived along contented, and banished pain and grief,
We had not occasion then to ask parish relief;
But now my hairs are grown quite grey, I cannot well engage
To work as I had used to do - I'm ninety years of age.

9. But now that I'm ninety years of age, and poverty do feel,
If for relief do go, they shove me in a Whig Bastille,
Where I may hang my weary head, and pine in grief and woe,
My father did not see the like, just ninety years ago.

10. When a man has laboured all his life, to do his country good,
He's respected just as much when old as a donkey in a wood,
His days are gone and past, and he may weep in grief and woe,
The times are very different now, to ninety years ago.

ONE MAN WENT TO MOW

5. Five men went to mow,
 Went to mow a meadow,
 Five men, four men, three men,
 two men, one man and his dog,
 Went to mow a meadow.

6. Six men went to mow,
 Went to mow a meadow,
 Six men, five men, four men, three men,
 two men, one man and his dog,
 Went to mow a meadow.

7. Seven men went to mow,
 Went to mow a meadow,
 Seven men, six men, five men, four men,
 three men, two men, one man and his dog,
 Went to mow a meadow,

8. Eight men went to mow,
 Went to mow a meadow,
 Eight men, seven men, six men, five men, four men,
 three men, two men, one man and his dog,
 Went to mow a meadow.

SHUCKIN' OF THE CORN

C
sold.
time.
I'm a - go - in' to the shuck - in' of the
corn,
I'm a - go - in' to the shuck - in' of the
G7
C
C7
F
corn,
A - shuck - in' of the corn and a - blow - in' of the
F#dim
C/G
G7
C
(D.C.)
horn, I'm a - go - in' to the shuck - in' of the corn.

THE VILLAGE BLACKSMITH

Words by Henry Wadsworth Longfellow
Music by W.H. Weiss

Guitar Tacet
E/D
Am/C
C7
B
Em
G7/F
hair is crisp and black and long, his face is like the tan. His
C/E
G7/D
C
G7/B
C
E7
Am7
D7
G7
C7-5
F
G/F
brow is wet with hon - est sweat, he earns what - e'er he can, And
C/E
G7/D
C
E/B
Am
F#dim
C/G
G7
C
C/E
looks the whole world in the face, for he owes not an - y man.
F
C/E
Dm7
C
Dm/F
C/G
G7
C

TURKEY IN THE STRAW

3. Met Mr. Catfish comin' down stream,
 Says Mr. Catfish, "What does you mean?"
 Caught Mr. Catfish by the snout
 And turned Mr. Catfish wrong side out.
 Chorus:

4. Came to the river and I couldn't get across,
 Paid five dollars for an old blind hoss
 Wouldn't go ahead, nor he wouldn't stand still,
 So he went up and down like an old saw mill.
 Chorus:

5. As I came down the new cut road
 Met Mr. Bullfrog, met Miss Toad,
 And every time Miss Toad would sing
 Ole Bullfrog cut a pigeon wing.
 Chorus:

6. Oh, I jumped in the seat, and I gave a little yell,
 The horses run away, broke the wagon all to hell;
 Sugar in the gourd and honey in the horn,
 I never was so happy since the hour I was born.
 Chorus:

CHORUS
Turkey in the straw, turkey in the hay,
Roll 'em up and twist 'em up a high tuckahaw,
And hit 'em up a tune called Turkey in the Straw.

THE WASHING DAY

2. My Kate, she is a bonny wife,
There's none so free from evil
Unless upon a washing day,
And then she is the devil!
The very kittens on the (h) earth
They dare not even play,
Away they jump with many a bump
Upon the washing day,
For 'tis thump, etc.

3. I met a friend who ask'd of me,
"How long's poor Kate been dead?"
Lamenting the good creature, gone
And sorry I was wed
To such a scolding vixen, while
He had been far away!
The truth it was, he chanced to come
Upon a washing day!
When 'tis scrub, scrub, etc.

4. I ask'd him then, to come and dine,
"Come, come." quoth I, "Ods buds!
I'll no denial take, you must;
Tho' Kate be in the suds!"
But what we had to dine upon,
In truth I cannot say,
But I think he'll never come again,
Upon a washing day!
When 'tis scrub, scrub, etc.

5. On that sad morning, when I rise,
I put a fervent prayer,
To all the gods, that it may be
Throughout the day quite fair!
That not a Cap or Handkerchief
May in the ditch be laid
For should it happen so egad,
I get a broken head!
For 'tis thump, thump, etc.

6. Old Homer sang a royal wash,
Down by a crystal river;
For dabbling in the palace halls
The king permitted never
On high Olympus, Beauty's queen
Such troubles well may scout,
While Jove and Juno with their train
Put all their washing out!
Ah! happy gods, they fear no sound,
Of thump and scold away;
But smile to view the perils of
A mortal washing day!

SCHOOL-DAYS

Words and music by Will D. Cobb and Gus Edwards

Fm/Ab G7 C7/4
hick - 'ry stick. You were my queen in cal - i -
C7 F F7/Eb Bb
co, I was your bash - ful, bare - foot beau, And you
Eb C#dim Bb/D Cm6/Eb D7 Bbm/Db
wrote on my slate, "I love you, Joe," When
rall.
C7 F7 Bb
we were a cou - ple of kids.
slower

YOUNG MAN WHO WOULDN'T HOE CORN

3. He went down to his neighbor's door
 Where he had been many times before;
 Pretty little miss, will you marry me,
 Pretty little miss, what do you say?

4. Well, here you air a-wantin' for to wed
 And cannot make your own corn bread.
 Single I be, single I remain;
 A lazy man I won't maintain.

5. Now go down to that cute little widder,
 And I hope that you don't git her.
 She gave him the mitten as sure as you're born,
 Because this young man wouldn't hoe corn.

IN HARVEST TIME (detail)

APPLE BUTTER MAKING

WORK FOR THE NIGHT IS COMING

Words by Ann L. Walker-Coghill
Music by Lowell Mason

A LITTLE PLAY

GRANDMA MOSES GOING TO BIG CITY

THE BIG ROCK CANDY MOUNTAIN

C
Dm7
C/E
Dm7
hon - ey, Where a bum can stay for many - y a day and he
heart - ed, Where you don't change socks and they don't throw rocks and your
C
G7
C
G7
C
won't need an - y mon - ey.
hair is nev - er part - ed.
Oh, the buzz - in' of the bees in the
F
C
cig - a - rette trees near the so - da wa - ter foun - tain, At the
Dm7
G7
C
Dm7
G7
C
(D.S.)
lem - on - ade springs where the blue - bird sings on the Big Rock Can - dy Moun - tain.

DO-RE-MI

Words by Oscar Hammerstein II
Music by Richard Rodgers

C
Me a name I call my - self,
G9
Far a long long way to run,
C/E
C7
F
Sew a nee - dle pull - ing thread,
D7
G
La a note to fol - low sew,

E7
Am
C
Tea a drink with jam and bread, That will
Fmaj7
Dm7
G7
1
C
bring us back to do - oh - oh - oh!
2
C
C7
F
Dm7
G7
doe! Do - re - mi - fa - so - la - ti -
C
do!
8va
8va

THE YELLOW BIRDS

FROSTY THE SNOW MAN

Words and music by Steve Nelson and Jack Rollins

Dm7 G7 C G7+5 C Cmaj7
eyes made out of coal. Frost - y the
fore I melt a - way. Down to the
C7 F E♭dim C/E
Snow man is a fair - y tale they say. He was
vil - lage with a broom - stick in his hand, Run - ning
F E♭dim Em7 A7 Dm7 G7
made of snow but the chil - dren know how he came to life one
here and there all a - round the square say - in', "Catch me if you
C F♯m7-5 Fm7 Em7 A7
day. There must have been some mag - ic in that
can." He led them down the streets of town right
more smoothly

Dm7 G7 Cmaj7 G/D
old silk hat they found, For when they placed it
to the traf - fic cop, And he on - ly paused a
G#dim D7 G13 G7+5
on his head he be - gan to dance a - round. Oh,
mo - ment when he heard him hol - ler, "Stop!" For
C Cmaj7 C7 F Ebdim
Frost - y the Snow man was a - live as he could
Frost - y the Snow man had to hur - ry on his
C/E F Ebdim Em7 A7
be, And the chil - dren say he could laugh and play just the
way, But he waved good - bye say - in', "Don't you cry; I'll be

Dm7
G7
1
C
G7+5
2
C
Guitar Tacet
same as you and me.
back a - gain some
day."
C
Thump - et - y thump thump, thump - et - y thump thump,
lightly
G7
look at Frost - y go!
Thump-et - y thump thump,
G
D
G7
C
thump-et - y thump thump, o - ver the hills of snow!

I DON'T WANT TO PLAY IN YOUR YARD

Words by Philip Wingate
Music by H.W. Petrie

F/A
Fm/A♭
C
G7
You'll be sor - ry when you see me slid - ing down our cel - lar
C
F
C7
door. You can't hol - ler down our rain - barrel
poco rit.
a tempo
F
E7+5
E♭7(no 5th)
D7
you can't climb our ap - ple tree. I don't wan - na play in
Gm
C7
F
your yard if you won't be good to me.

JACK AND JILL

JACK AND JILL

MARY AND LITTLE LAMB

MARY HAD A LITTLE LAMB

Words by Sarah J. Hale

3. It followed her to school one day,
 School one day, school one day.
 It followed her to school one day
 Which was against the rule.

4. It made the children laugh and play,
 Laugh and play, laugh and play.
 It made the children laugh and play
 To see a lamb at school.

5. So the teacher turned it out,
 Turned it out, turned it out.
 So the teacher turned it out,
 But still it lingered near.

IN MY MERRY OLDSMOBILE

Words by Vincent Bryan
Music by Gus Edwards

C7
Cdim
C7
road of life we'll fly, au - to - mo -
F
F#dim
C7
bub - bling, you and I. To the
F
D7
church we'll swift - ly steal,
G7
then our wed - ding bells will

C7
peal. You can go as
C/B♭
F/A
Dm
far as you like with me in my
G7
C7
F
F♯dim
mer - ry Olds - mo - bile.
C7
F
F♯dim
C7
F
Come a bile.

THE OLD AUTOMOBILE

THE SKATERS

Moderate Waltz
C
G7
p
simile
Cmaj7
Am
Dm7
G7
melody
1 and Fine
C
Fine
2
C
pp

G7
C
1
Em
B7
Em
G7
2
C7
F
Fm6
C/G
G7
C
D.C. al Fine

LITTLE BROWN JUG

Words and music by Eastburn (Joseph Eastburn Winner)

2. 'Tis you who makes my friends my foes,
'Tis you who makes me wear old clothes,
Here you are so near my nose,
So tip her up and down she goes.

3. When I go toiling to my farm,
I take little brown jug under my arm
I place it under a shady tree,
Little brown jug 'tis you and me.

4. If all the folks in Adam's race,
Were gather'd together in one place,
Then I'd prepare to shed a tear,
Before I part from you, my dear.

5. If I'd a cow that gave such milk
I'd clothe her in the finest silk;
I'd feed her on the choicest hay,
And milk her forty times a day.

THE TREE IN THE WOOD

5. And in this nest there was an egg, etc.

6. And in this egg there was a bird, etc.

7. And on this bird there was a wing, etc.

8. And on this wing there was a feather, etc.

YEAR 1860 AND YEAR 1940

TITLE INDEX

Anna Mary Robertson Moses, famous as "Grandma Moses," was born in 1860 in New York State and died there (at Eagle Bridge) in 1961, but spent twenty years in Virginia, where her ten children were born. Her education, in a one-room schoolhouse, ended when she was twelve, and she worked as a hired girl until her marriage to a farmer. She lived all her life on a farm and began to paint only after her husband had died and her five surviving children were grown. She was then in her seventies. Her pictures of life in rural America, the changing seasons, and the daily chores and pleasures of farming, have met with ever-wider response in the years since her first solo exhibition, held in 1940 at the Galerie St. Etienne in New York.

Dan Fox has long been active on the New York music scene. He has arranged songs for some of the greatest pop stars of the last twenty years and has also arranged and edited many of the most successful songbooks, as well as scores of instruction books, choral works and band pieces. In his specially commissioned arrangements of the music for The Grandma Moses Songbook, he has admirably succeeded in making the songs relatively simple to play while at the same time retaining their effectiveness and tonal color.